I0866686

OPEN & GROW

small group study

Stressed Out Leader Guide

A Practical Biblical Approach to Anxiety

Todd Friel

New Leaf Press
A Division of New Leaf Publishing Group
www.newleafpress.net

First printing: August 2016

New Leaf Press, P.O. Box 726, Green Forest, AR 72638

New Leaf Press is a division of the New Leaf Publishing Group, Inc.

ISBN: 978-0-89221-746-5

Unless otherwise noted, Scripture quotations are from the New King James Version of the Bible.

Please consider requesting that a copy of this volume be purchased by your local library system.

Printed in the United States of America

Please visit our website for other great titles:
www.newleafpress.net

For information regarding author interviews,
please contact the publicity department at (870) 438-5288

New Leaf Press
A Division of New Leaf Publishing Group
www.newleafpress.net

Course Overview: Stressed Out?

Through *Stressed Out* in 5 sessions. Session Length: 60–90 minutes. Set includes DVD, Leaders Guide, *Stressed Out* book. Participants are encouraged to read the book alongside the course.

Notes to Leader

Dear Teacher:

Let me congratulate you for your willingness to help people battle the common malady of anxiety. Most people limp through life feeling the anchor of anxiety chained to their ankle. You are endeavoring to help fellow believers lead the joy-filled Christian life that Jesus promises. You are to be applauded.

Let me share a few suggestions on how to maximize your time with this study.

1. Please read the appropriate chapters in the book BEFORE each class. If not, read it after the class, but whatever you do, read it! You will get the most out of this if you dive into the book itself. It is suggested that participants have the book, *Stressed Out*, prior to beginning the study and have read chapters 1–4.

2. If you fail to read the assigned chapters for the week, don't stress out and don't quit. You will still get a lot out of the class. I promise.
3. Watch the short video before answering each chapter's questions. Some of the questions have suggested or objective answers provided, while others are more open ended. Also, there is room for notes to add your own questions or customize the session.

Play Video

---

4. There is a time and place for sharing long stories, but discipline yourself and everyone else in the class to not turn each question into lengthy diatribes. Stay focused on the question. I encourage you to remind the class of that rule before you begin each week. Teacher, you will have to use your discretion as to when you let someone talk for a long time. If you find yourself struggling to cut someone off, lovingly say, "I hate to interrupt, but in order to stay on schedule with all of the material, could you share that at the end of class if there is time?"

Begin Discussion: 10–15 min.

---

5. If someone chooses to debate a particular teaching, that is fine, just make it a biblical discussion. Use Scripture to address questions or confusion. Ask questions like, "How does your comment/position/understanding align with this verse?"
6. It is not impossible that someone might become emotional during a class. Take your time to help them through it. If it appears it may take a while, perhaps you could have someone from your class go to a private place to work through the issue.

7. It is not only possible but likely that someone in your class is anxious because he or she is simply not saved. It would be wise to regularly remind your class about the gospel and repentance and genuine saving faith. It is biblical to challenge people to examine themselves to see if they are in the faith. Don't be a fruit inspector, but don't overlook the reality that there are usually goats mingled with the sheep. Shepherd them lovingly and biblically.
8. Watch your time! Keep the class on schedule so you can get through all of the prescribed chapters for the week. Should you miss a chapter, don't worry.
9. Pray before and after each class based on the Bible verses and content of the chapters covered. If you have time, you will find it helpful to write out your prayers in advance. The more you load your prayers with Bible truths, the more powerful your prayers will be. You might find it helpful to take notes during the class if someone confesses to a particular struggle or challenge; that way you can incorporate their need in your closing prayer.

May God bless you as you dive into the Bible to see the power of His Word at work in the lives of His saints. And one more time: way to go!

Session 1

Understanding Anxiety

Begin Session 1. Understanding Anxiety (60–90 minutes)

Welcome! We are about to begin a five-part study on stress and look at the biblical approach to anxiety. We all have it — what do we do with it?

Play Session 1. Video — Chapter 1: Welcome, Intro and Your Issue (5 min.)

Begin Discussion: 10–15 min.

Chapter One Discussion Questions:

1. Does knowing you are not the only anxious person on the planet help you to not feel anxious?

Notes: ____

____

2. What does God want to do with your anxiety?

   Answer: Use you to conform you into the image of His Son.

Notes: ____

____

3. There are four reasons some people never want to get well (they don't think they are sick, they like the attention illness brings, they are comfortable, or they are not willing to try to get better). Do any of these excuses possibly apply to your anxiety?

Notes:

4. Please take the time with the book to thoughtfully consider if you might have a genuine (albeit rare) organic depression (a black dog that howls) or if you are simply struggling with the issue the Bible calls "being troubled."

Notes:

5. Can you explain why the person with organic depression still needs to battle anxiety even if he or she takes medication?
Answer: Because medicine does not change our hearts or sinful propensities. Medication may give you the ability to address your stress, but only a concerted effort to defeat anxiety will ultimately cure you.

Notes:

Okay, let's watch Todd's next video, Your Thinking.

Play Session 1. Video — Chapter 2: Your Thinking (5 min.)

Begin Discussion: 10–15 min.

Chapter Two Discussion Questions:

1. Do you think you might have done a better job than Adam in representing the entire human race?
Answer: No. None of us would have resisted the temptation Adam gave into.

Notes:

2. Thomas Watson's quote is a very difficult and profound statement. Do you agree with Thomas Watson that God actually afflicts you with difficult situations in order to "draw Christ's image more distinctly on us"?

Notes:

3. Based on 2 Corinthians 12:9–10, do you agree with the statement, "God never gives you more than you can handle"?
   Answer: No. It is quite clear that God uses our weakness to demonstrate His strength.

Notes: ____

____

4. This is another profound and difficult statement: anxiety, at its core, is nothing more than garden-variety sinning. Do you agree?
   Answer: Yes. When Jesus commands us to "not be troubled," then we are disobeying His commandment to not be anxious.

Notes: ____

____

5. As difficult as it may be to swallow the pill that says "your anxiety is a sin problem," can you explain why that truth should not crush you, but actually give you hope?
   Answer: When God commands us to do something, He always gives us the power and the tools to be obedient. That means that your sinful anxiety is absolutely overcome-able.

Notes: ____

____

Let's watch Todd's next video, Your Anxiety.

Play Session 1. Video — Chapter 3: Your Anxiety (5 min.)

Begin Discussion: 10–15 min.

Chapter Three Discussion Questions:

1. Has anyone ever told you to stop mourning a loss? Was he or she right or wrong to tell you to "just get over it"?

Notes:

2. If someone you know is sad because of the loss of a loved one, do you need to make him or her sadness go away?
Answer: No. We should let him or her mourn.

Notes:

3. If a friend or loved one is sad because of the loss of a loved one, can you see how simply "mourning with those who mourn" might be the best thing you can do?

Notes:

4. Can non-sinful mourning ever become sinful? If so, how?
Answer: Yes; if the mourning is protracted (a very difficult thing to determine based on the situation and the loss), or if the mourning becomes self-absorbed, attention seeking, or lacking in any hope.

Notes:

5. There are many things that can cause us to be sad (death, a loss, an unfulfilled hope, prodigal children). Where is the line between non-sinful mourning and sinful mourning?
Answer: Being disappointed is a natural, human response to a loss, tragedy, or disappointment. We should feel free to mourn those events. But if your mourning is based on entitlement, anger with God, frustration, hopelessness, a sense that God does not care or ever do good things for you, then it is sinful mourning.

Notes:

Now, let's watch Todd's next video, Your God.

Play Session 1. Video — Chapter 4: Your God (5 min.)

Begin Discussion: 10–15 min.

Chapter Four Discussion Questions:

1. When God says that He is for us, is that a promise that only good things will happen in this life?
   Answer: No. It is a promise that God will do the very best things FOR us to accomplish His purposes for us.

Notes:

2. Here is another difficult statement: "God does not give you the life you want; God gives you the life you need." Do you agree with that statement? If so, how might that bring you comfort the next time God does something difficult FOR you?

Notes:

3. Consider the statement, "If you are in Christ, your biggest problem has been solved: all of your sins are forgiven." Why is that statement true?
Answer: Because nothing is worse than facing the wrath of God for our sins.

Notes: ______________________________

____

4. How might that statement comfort you the next time a temporal difficulty arises?
Answer: It can give us an eternal and spiritual perspective as opposed to a mere temporal and physical perspective. It seems silly to mourn over a sliver in your finger when your life has just been saved.

Notes: ______________________________

____

5. When was the last time you pondered that God is FOR you? When was the last time you pondered how amazing grace is? How might you spend more time remembering those things in the future?

Notes: ______________________________

____

End Session 1. To the group: To prepare for the next session, please be sure to read through chapter 8 in the book *Stressed Out*.

Notes:

Session 2
Anxiety Relievers, 1–4

Begin Session 2. Anxiety Relievers, 1–4 (60–90 minutes) Welcome! We are about to begin session two of a five-part study on stress and look at the biblical approach to anxiety. In the last session we defined anxiety and its diagnosis. In this session, we will look at four anxiety relievers.

Play Session 2. Video — Chapter 5: Anxiety Reliever #1: You Have a Diagnosis (5 min.)

Begin Discussion: 10–15 min.

Chapter Five Discussion Questions:

1. Ouch. Does it sting a little bit to know that your anxiety is actually a lack of faith?

Notes:

2. Do you see the connection between lack of trust and anxiety?

Notes:

3. Does "having a little faith" mean you are not saved?
   Answer: No. It means that in the moment, you are simply not trusting God and His promises to you.

Notes: ______________________________

____

4. Can you recreate the secular versus the Christian train of thinking?
   Answer: The secular train puts thinking first, followed by actions and then emotions. The Christian train puts faith first, followed by thinking, then actions and emotions.

Notes: ______________________________

____

5. Peter sank because he lacked faith in Jesus. Similarly, when we are anxious, we are not trusting God the way we should. Think of the last time you were stressed out. What were you trusting? Self? Spouse? Children's success? Money? Personal skills? Luck? Personal attributes? An investment firm? A strong economy? Other?

Notes: ______________________________

____

Let's watch Todd's next video, You Have a Future.

Play Session 2. Video — Chapter 6: Anxiety Reliever #2: You have a future (5 min.)

Begin Discussion: 10–15 min.

Chapter Six Discussion Questions:

1. Be honest — were you thinking about the glories of heaven the last time you were worried about a future event?

Notes:

2. How can our anxiety help us know where our priorities are? *Answer: We worry about what we love the most. If we worry about temporal things, that means our hearts are set on the here and now instead of the there and then. Anxiety can help reveal the idols in our hearts.*

Notes:

3. Do you see how thinking about our future hope can help us cope with our temporal struggles? Imagine what life would be like without heaven to look forward to.

Notes:

4. You are going to reign with Christ (2 Timothy 2:11–12). How could you apply that truth the next time someone shames, slanders, hates, or disappoints you?
   Answer: Who cares what the servants think when the King says, "You are mine. I have prepared a place just for you."

Notes:

5. How could you think about heaven more?
   Answer: Read the Bible's promises about heaven, and grow in your understanding of the joys that await us.

Notes:

Now, let's watch Todd's next video, You Know God.

Play Session 2. Video — Chapter 7: Anxiety Reliever #3: You Know God (5 min.)

Begin Discussion: 10–15 min.

Chapter Seven Discussion Questions:

1. How does it feel to know God?

Notes:

2. How does it feel to be known and loved by God?

Notes:

3. Take a look at your address book. Do any of those names compare to the name of Jesus Christ?

Notes:

4. How could you use this knowledge the next time you are anxious about not living a glamorous life, or being famous, or knowing celebrities?

Notes: ____________________

____

5. How could you use this knowledge the next time you are feeling the weight of peer pressure?
   Answer: Once again, who cares what the servants think when I know the King, and I know that He loves me.

Notes: ____________________

____

Okay, let's watch Todd's next video, You can hear from God.

Play Session 2. Video — Chapter 8: Anxiety Reliever #4: You Can Hear from God (5 min.)

Begin Discussion: 10–15 min.

Chapter Eight Discussion Questions

1. Based on 2 Timothy 3:16–17, do you agree that the Bible is absolutely, unquestionably the only source of communication we need from God for life and godliness?

Notes: ______

______

2. What are the two major themes we see in Psalm 119?
   Answer: The Psalmist was facing a serious threat or danger. He believed the Word was the cure to his anxiety.

Notes: ______

______

3. Can any of the following activities actually turn your anxiety into joy? A day at the spa, a cruise, a weekend at the beach.
Answer: These perfectly fine activities might distract you or take your mind off your worries, but your problems will still be there when you are done getting your pedicure.

Notes: ____

____

4. Based on 2 Corinthians 3:18; Colossians 3:9–10; 2 Peter 1:2–4; 2 Timothy 3:16–17, what is God's authorized means for growing us in holiness, peace, and joy?
Answer: The Word of God.

Notes: ____

____

5. How does studying Jesus make us more like Jesus?
Answer: The Word says so. While it may or may not be true that you are what you eat, you will become what you focus on and worship.

Notes: ____

____

End Session 2. To the group: To prepare for the next session, please be sure to read through chapter 12 in the book *Stressed Out*.

Notes:

Session 3
Anxiety Relievers, 5–8

Begin Session 3. Anxiety Relievers, 5–8 (60–90 minutes) Welcome! We are about to begin session three of a five-part study on stress and look at the biblical approach to anxiety. In the last session we looked at four anxiety relievers. They were:

1. You have a diagnosis.
2. You have a future.
3. You know God.
4. You can hear from God.

In this session we are going to look at four more anxiety relievers. Let's start by watching Todd talk about Anxiety Reliever # 5, You Have a Comforter.

Play Session 3. Video — Chapter 9: Anxiety Reliever #5: You Have a Comforter (5 min.)

Begin Discussion: 10–15 min.

Chapter Five Discussion Questions:

1. What are some of the ways different Bible versions translate the word "Helper" in John 14:16?
   Answer: Comforter, Counselor, Advocate.

Notes: ______________________________

____

2. According to John 14:16, when does the Holy Spirit leave you?
Answer: He doesn't. He promises to "never leave you."

Notes: ___

3. Knowing that you have the same power in you that worked in Jesus Christ to fulfill all righteousness, have you been accessing that power when you have been anxious?

Notes: ___

4. How does the Holy Spirit typically work to comfort or counsel you?
Answer: Through the Word, which He inspired (John 16:5–15).

Notes: ___

5. When Romans 8 tells us that we are to be led by the Holy Spirit, does the context of chapter 8 tell us what that means?
Answer: Yes. If you read the entire chapter, it clearly means that the Holy Spirit leads us as we become increasingly saturated in the Word. Romans 8 does not teach that the Holy Spirit leads us through promptings, nudgings, or liver shivers.

Notes: ___

Okay, let's watch Todd's next video, You Are Going to Get a New Body.

Play Session 3. Video — Chapter 10: Anxiety Reliever #6: You Are Going to Get a New Body (5 min.)

Begin Discussion: 10–15 min.

Chapter Six Discussion Questions:

1. Take a moment to consider how it feels to know that you are not really going to die.

Notes:

2. Take another moment to ponder what it will be like to get a new, improved body that will last for all eternity without a single ache, pain, or malfunction. Ever.

Notes:

3. Take a third moment to consider the amount of pain you would have suffered if Jesus had not taken the judgment of God on your behalf.

Notes:

4. What absolute assurance do you have that you are going to get an amazing new body that will never wear out? With that knowledge, should you ever fear death?
   Answer: Because Jesus is the first fruits of the Resurrection (1 Corinthians 15:20). We should no longer fear death because it has been swallowed up in victory (1 Corinthians 15:53–57).

Notes:

5. How can Jesus' promise of a new, resurrected body help you through your next bout of the flu, chemotherapy, a stiff knee, tennis elbow, headaches, or fibromyalgia?

Notes:

Now, let's watch Todd's next video, You Have Real Peace.

Play Session 3. Video — Chapter 11: Anxiety Reliever #7: You Have Real Peace (5 min.)

Begin Discussion: 10–15 min.

Chapter Six Discussion Questions:

1. If Jesus is the only way to true peace, is it appropriate to consider every other promise of peace a lie?
   Answer: Yes.

Notes:

2. Do you agree with this statement? "If you are not happy in a 1,500 square foot home, you won't be happy in 15,000 square foot home."

Notes:

3. Could pondering your crimes against God, which were paid for by Jesus, help you appreciate the peace you have been given? How?

Notes:

4. When considering the cup of wrath that Jesus drank for us, does that knowledge give you perspective on earthly woes? How?

Notes:

5. Can you explain how true peace is directly linked to your salvation? *Answer: The knowledge that my biggest problem has been solved gives me peace that surpasses understanding.*

Notes:

Let's watch Todd's next video, You Have an Avenger.

Play Session 3. Video — Chapter 12: Anxiety Reliever #8: You Have an Avenger (5 min.)

Begin Discussion: 10–15 min.

Chapter Six Discussion Questions:

1. Think about the people who have sinned against you throughout your life. Who has wounded you in such a profound way that you cannot get over it? Do you harbor anger toward that person or even God?

Notes:

2. What is God going to do with the unsaved sinners who have hurt you? *Answer: He is going to utterly destroy them for eternity in hell.*

Notes:

3. Do you think you could do a better job than God of avenging the wrongs committed against you? Should this give you the ability to stop harboring bitterness or hatred?

Notes:

4. Take some to think about the fate of your enemies. What will it be like for them on the Day of Judgment? What will it be like for them after ten thousand years of eternal conscious torment? Can you see how spending time pondering the fate of the ungodly could actually move you from anger to pity and even love for your enemies?

Notes:

5. Imagine that your enemy repents and trusts Jesus Christ for his/her salvation. Can you be satisfied in knowing that the sins that have been committed against you will have been absorbed by Jesus when He died on a Cross for those sins?

Notes:

End Session 3. To the group: To prepare for the next session, please be sure to read through chapter 16 in the book *Stressed Out*.

Notes:

Session 4

Anxiety Relievers, 9–12

Begin Session 4. Anxiety Relievers, 9–12 (60–90 minutes) Welcome! We are about to begin session four of a five-part study on stress and look at the biblical approach to anxiety. So far we have looked at eight anxiety relievers. They were:

1. You have a diagnosis.
2. You have a future.
3. You know God.
4. You can hear from God.
5. You have a Comforter.
6. You are going to get a new body.
7. You have real peace.
8. You have an avenger.

In this session we are going to look at four more anxiety relievers. Let's start by watching Todd talk about Anxiety Reliever # 9. You Have a Father who lovingly disciplines.

Play Session 4. Video — Chapter 13: Anxiety Reliever #9: You Have an Avenger (5 min.)

Begin Discussion: 10–15 min.

Chapter Five Discussion Questions:

1. Does God ever discipline you in anger?
   Answer: No. He only lovingly disciplines those He loves.

Notes:

2. Think about a recent trial you have endured. Did you learn anything from it? Why or why not? Did you grow in holiness because of it? Why or why not?

Notes: ____

3. Who gets the responsibility for the non-sinful calamities that happen in your life? Who gets the responsibility for the sinful calamities that happen in your life?
Answer: God. The sinner who committed the sin.

Notes:

4. This may be one of the most difficult statements in the entire book: "God causes all non-sinful calamities, and He permits sinful calamities. Either way, all events are ultimately under God's sovereign control." Do you agree with that statement? Please support your position by using Bible verses. Do you see how this knowledge can better help you respond to tragedies?

Notes:

5. If God were capricious, mean, or short-tempered, the doctrine of sovereignty would be horrifying. But our loving God only disciplines in love, because He knows what is absolutely best for us. Can you live with that truth? Can you embrace that truth? Can you find comfort in that truth?

Notes:

Okay, let's watch Todd's next video, You Have a Pre-arranged Plan.

Play Session 4. Video — Chapter 14: Anxiety Reliever #10: You Have a Pre-arranged Plan (5 min.)

Begin Discussion: 10–15 min.

Chapter Fourteen Discussion Questions:

1. How can acknowledging our complete dependence on Jesus for everything actually be a comfort?
   Answer: Because Jesus always knows what is best and does what is finest. We don't.

Notes:

2. Does God ever get informed about a hurricane, tornado, or earthquake?
   Answer: No, He caused them.

Notes:

3. Imagine your neighbor's home has no roof damage from the hailstorm, but your roof needs to be replaced. How can the doctrine of God's perfect sovereignty help you accept the bad news?

Notes:

4. Can you think of a time when you, like Joseph, went through something very difficult but could look back and see that God had His hand all over it?

Notes:

5. If God does not give us the life we want, but only the life we need to become more like His Son, Jesus Christ, can you live with the lot that God has tailor-made for you and your family? Could this knowledge help you and your children not grumble, be embarrassed, or covet a fancier lifestyle?

Notes:

Now, let's watch Todd's next video, Anxiety Reliever #11: You Can Talk to God.

Play Session 4. Video — Chapter 14: Anxiety Reliever #11: You Can Talk to God (5 min.)

Begin Discussion: 10–15 min.

Chapter Fifteen Discussion Questions:

1. When something goes wrong that can lead to stress, who is the first person you typically talk to? Who should be the first one you go to? *Answer to second question: God.*

Notes:

2. Does God promise that we will not be anxious if we pray to Him? *Answer: Yes (Philippians 4:6–7).*

Notes:

3. Do you have a tendency to cast your cares on God, but reel them back in and keep worrying about them? Should you? How could you stop doing this?

Notes:

4. What is the difference between prayers and supplications? Are we supposed to do both?
Answer: Prayers include thanks, confession, repentance, and praise. Supplications are requests. We should offer both prayers and supplications.

Notes:

5. Why do you think that praying with praise and thanksgiving actually gives us joy when we are worried?
Answer: It replaces grumbling with gratitude as we focus on the good things that God has done for us.

Notes:

Let's watch Todd's next video, Anxiety Reliever #12: Your God Loves You.

Play Session 4. Video — Chapter 16: Anxiety Reliever #12: Your God Loves You (5 min.)

Begin Discussion: 10–15 min.

Chapter Sixteen Discussion Questions:

1. Spend some time thinking about how you have been loved throughout your life. Have you felt truly loved? Have you experienced more animosity than love? Do you wish that you had been loved more?

Notes:

2. How do we know, beyond the shadow of a doubt that God loves us? *Answer: He sent His Son to die for us while we were yet sinning (Romans 5:8).*

Notes:

3. Here is another saying that can wound our pride: God does not love us because we are lovable. How can this knowledge bring us comfort and security?
Answer: Knowing that God's love for us is based on His nature and not our performance means we are secure in His love. We don't have to perform to earn God's love; He loves us because He loves us. What a relief.

Notes: ______________________________

____

4. We should appreciate God's love more as we ponder how sinful we are. How much time have you spent pondering your own depravity? Would it help you to know you are loved profoundly by considering your own wickedness? Might that knowledge help you grow in your appreciation for God's love for you in Christ?

Notes: ______________________________

____

5. If you are in Christ, can God's love for you ever waver based on your performance?
Answer: No. God always loves us with the same amount of love He has for His Son.

Notes: ______________________________

____

End Session 4. To the group: To prepare for the next session, please be sure to read through chapter 18 in the book *Stressed Out*.

Notes:

Session 5
Let the Healing Begin

Begin Session 5. Let the Healing Begin (60–90 minutes)
Welcome! We are about to begin our last session of our study on stress and the biblical approach to anxiety. So far we have looked at 12 anxiety relievers. They were:

1. You have a diagnosis.
2. You have a future.
3. You know God.
4. You can hear from God.
5. You have a Comforter.
6. You are going to get a new body.
7. You have real peace.
8. You have an avenger.
9. You have a Father who lovingly disciplines.
10. You have a pre-arranged plan.
11. You can talk to God.
12. Your God loves you.

In this session we are going wrap up this study with an action plan for overcoming stress and anxiety. Let's start by watching Todd talk about Your Goal.

Play Session 5. Video — Chapter 17: Your Goal (5 min.)

Begin Discussion: 10–15 min.

Chapter Seventeen Discussion Questions:

1. Were you surprised to learn that the goal of this book was not to simply remove your anxiety, but to give you biblical reasons to love Him, serve Him, and glorify Him better?

Notes:

2. In John 15:9–11, Jesus said that if you keep His commandments, your joy will be full. Do you see how focusing on glorifying God replaces anxiety with joy?

Notes:

3. Sanctification is a process, not an event. Should you expect to lose all of your anxiety over night? Should you be discouraged the next time you are anxious? If you are in Christ, should you ever feel guilty?
Answer: Sin is not an "if" question, it is a "when" question. Knowing that sanctification is a process helps us respond rightly when we sin. It is perfectly right to feel remorse for our sins, but it is not right to feel guilty, because we are not guilty anymore, thanks to Jesus.

Notes:

4. What does it mean to "continue in Jesus' Word" (John 8:31–32)? How should this knowledge change how much/often we read our Bibles?
Answer: We continue in His Word by reading, heeding, and obeying God's Word continually. Knowing that our source of joy, peace, happiness, and contentment is found only in the Word should cause us to desire it more and more.

Notes:

5. Can you expect to have peace when you do not read your Bible, hear biblical sermons, fellowship with believers, take communion regularly, witness baptisms, and pray? Why or why not?
Answer: No; you can only expect anxiety. If you do not plug into God's power source, you will have only worry and woe, not peace and joy.

Notes:

Okay, let's watch Todd's next video, Your Plan — Wrap up and Commission.

Play Session 5. Video — Chapter 18: Your Plan — Wrap up and Commission (10 min.)

Begin Discussion: 25–35 min.

Chapter Eighteen Discussion Questions:

1. Would you be willing, right now, to spend some time thinking about how you need to change your language and repent of past sins of anxiety? Would it be a good idea to talk to your God about these issues right now?

Notes:

2. May I challenge you with a rather strong statement: if you do not hunger and thirst for God's Word, something is horribly wrong. You are either not saved, or you have been sinning and you need to repent. Do you?

Notes:

3. Take some time to consider your life and your schedule. What would be the best time to commit to reading your Bible every day? Do you have to adopt someone else's Bible reading plan and schedule? *Answer: No; create your own plan, and if that happens to be a prescribed plan that works for you, then go for it.*

Notes: ______________________________

____

4. Ray Comfort likes to say, "No read, no feed." In other words, if you are eating three meals a day but not reading your Bible, then your priorities are out of whack. Would you take a moment right now to consider if you need to repent of esteeming food more than the nourishment that comes from God's Word?

Notes: ______________________________

____

5. This may sound a little radical, but can I encourage you to not get an accountability partner? It is easy to lie and fall into the ditch of simply explaining away your lack of discipline. Instead, ask God for His help to get started and stay faithful. He is willing and able to complete that good work within you. Do you need to talk to Him now and ask Him for His help?

Notes: ______________________________

____